FINISHING LINE PRESS

www.finishinglinepress.com

Watercolors in the Desk Drawer

poems by

Georgette Unis

Finishing Line Press
Georgetown, Kentucky

Watercolors
in the Desk Drawer

Publisher: Leah Huete de Maines
Editor: Christen Kincaid
Cover Art: Water Series L#61 by Georgette Unis
Author Photo: Robert Walker
Cover Design: Elizabeth Maines McCleavy

Order online: www.finishinglinepress.com
              also available on amazon.com

Author inquiries and mail orders:
Finishing Line Press
P. O. Box 1626
Georgetown, Kentucky 40324
U. S. A.

Table of Contents

I. What Blossoms Will Spring

II. Planting Mint and Roses

III. Eye of A Wanderer

The artist will be held responsible
For something so far unsaid but true
                    Report from the Field by Dorthea Tanning

I

What Blossoms Will Spring

Perspective

My father smiles when
he touches my cheek,

peruses the studio
in a covert attempt to read

my sketchbook journals,
search for secrets I, too,

wish to understand.
I retrieve my notes,

offer to draw
his portrait instead,

enshrine his image
in a sculptural collage

along with his glasses,
the need for which

becomes his legacy
to me.

Reservoir

I pedal hard on the circular trail,
head forward, helmet heavy
against wind.
White filigrees flash
in my periphery
and I brake
to join other cyclists.
We line up on the wharf,
a colorful array in biking plumage,
to watch egrets flutter wings
and prance their feet
in graceful seductions.

Beside silver green water,
I cycle face to sun
anticipating curves
through high brush.
Crows rise, scatter
except for one,
gauges its speed to mine,
turns its head toward me
once, then again.
What have you come to tell me?
But it flies away as though
the question is its task.

The path becomes road,
its avian habitat secure
behind a metal gate.
I measure my skill to vehicles,
watch couples walk
through shaded grass
hip to hip,
coiffed in earbuds,
when their barking dog
runs beside me.

I meet the challenge.
No sanctuary here
but the strength of my legs.

A Surreal Memoir

Time bends
the chronometer,

a white horse
runs the distance

between here
and open space.

Gradations of
iron earth

and cerulean hues
hide the horizon.

Magnolia leaves
cover the grass

in August crisp,
crumple at sight.

The tree roots itself
in shadow,

its presence knowable
by circular winds.

A storm continues
in measures

of a second
handed clock,

ruffles the mane
of the equine

hungry for
its pasture,

as it searches
the ground.

Heritage

Your father teaches you to fish the side waters
of rapid rivers as his mother taught him

and your mother teaches you to prepare
your catch for supper,

absorb the grit of your ancestors
from patterns on your plate.

Your ambered hair curls as intently
as your mind absorbs actions around you.

Your indigo eyes glow
with the never-rest intelligence of starlight.

Each grandparent weaves blood red
fireweed into your curls and you learn

how to open a cactus in drought,
drink its salvaged water,

how to seal your boots before you cross
meadows soggy with other people's plans,

how to scale a granite mountain to carve
your own trail even if clouds descend on it

and you must then navigate blind in white light
but still celebrate where you stand.

Oracle

In honor of Georgia O'Keeffe, 1817-1989

She says
in my next life
I will be a singer
of high notes
clear
strong
soprano
notes

she knows
her age
lends itself
to alto tones
but she says
she will sing
anyway
and nothing will
hinder today's
desire

because
its substance
is not made
of this earth
but of stars
that renew
themselves

in the fire
of the Phoenix Bird
an eternal force
beyond mortal
ever singing
of a baby's birth
because the sun

will always rise
on an infant's
innocent hope

The Artists Circle

We paint landscapes
        of barren trees
        in tainted umber,

meet for coffee,
        talk of art

and how leaves do not grow
        in the winter soil of philosophies
        but rather along the arteries
            of unfortunates.

We insist in strident tones
        of the over-caffeinated
        classical form,
            color,
            composition
            and *beauty*
are chimeras,
        an apocalypse
        with a twist:
            those horses divine
            their own undoing.

When amber spirits
        soothe our rhetoric,
        we accept the golden mean
            as our gift to each other

before the moon rises
        and loneliness
            dims our mirth.

In Rilke's Shadow

*Love your solitude and bear with sweet-sounding
lamentation the suffering it causes you.*
Rainer Maria Rilke

Ceramic masks cover an entire wall;
shelves and counters laden with figures.

I formed them in all sizes, some delicate,
others wide-hipped and buxom,

some bald, some with wild hair
adorned in feathers, twigs

or beaded strings,
topped with fish or crows.

One resembles my aunt
who died young,

another, an uncle also gone.
Some faces belong to friends,

others evolved from fantasy.
 All eyes open, alert,

mouths prepared for conversation.
Silence a threshold toward solitude.

Would that I could be a Pygmalion
and make these sculptures breathe.

An Egret in Winter

Its white form statuesque, barely hidden
in pale reeds around the neighborhood pond.

Myriad trees whose leaves change
wardrobes from greens to dusty sage,

golden ocher, fire orange, now expose
their branches in nude grey.

No fish live in this miniature lake.
I suspect the egret waits for a frog or mouse,

feet submerged in murky water,
a place both physical and mental,

natural to creatures who find sustenance
in quiet moments, an art I wish to learn.

Fishing

Silver scaled fish
swim in a burbling river
seen only by the raptor's eye,

too deep for me to capture
as though I were a child,
homemade pole in hand

made of crooked stick
and kitchen string tied
to a squiggly earthworm.

My toes curl into garden soil
when a garter snake devours
a tiny mouse squirming,

reminds me how I tried
to unleash my brother's grip
after I taunted him

in front of his new girlfriend
then ran giggling behind bushes
where he nearly pummeled me.

Just before twilight opens its doors
I still have no fish to cook
and scrounge the vegetable patch

for beans and squash,
my orchard for a succulent peach,
its juice to dress my tongue,

while on the water's edge,
a heron moves without ripple
in its careful predatory prance.

Glacier Channel

words snooze
at sea bottom

would that they leap
over white capped waves

in a dolphin dance
paired and tripled

with smiles
and splashes

amid ice floe
alongside my ship

maybe tomorrow
they will surface

close enough
to fish

with lines
that glisten

like poems
in the light

Red Bud

The red buds live bare in winter
  though some trees keep their pods

otherwise stand thin
  against a cold sky.

A sleeping infant hears sounds
  familiar even before birth

and afterwards sees images
  of faces, colors, movements

then forms words that lighten the tongue
  challenge the mouth

as speech moves from bubbles
  to imitation to perspective

and I suspect meaning comes
  in company with all of that

I doubt a red bud
  ponders the possibilities

of its behavior before it blooms
  into a thousand tiny flowers

any more than a child knows
  what blossoms will spring

from the kaleidoscope
  language offers.

New Entries

This dark morning,
I drink my coffee with pills
and a throbbing headache.

Curled up on the sofa,
dim light over my right shoulder,
I read young poets' poems,

search for connection.
I could be mother
or grandmother to some.

Their issues current
on topics such as the dad
loved, but absent,

or bathroom humor
to tease the boy's teacher,
impress his buddies,

the girl's golden retriever
who licks away her tears
over Valentines not received.

Eloquently splayed
across the page,
their opened hearts

offer a serum I absorb
from their earnest craft,
their language more adept

than chemical relief
to ease my affliction
and raise the sun.

A Saturday in April

Today would have been a day for *Poetry in the Garden,*
an annual botanical fest, celebrated with readings

under the arbors of wisteria and fragrant jasmine,
accompanied by fountains bubbling over stones.

But the event is cancelled, not because of rain,
rather as strategy against a feral virus.

Poets' eloquence remains unspoken about spring air,
its scent of new roses, blue jay squawks against

the competition of bird song, buds and fledglings
in sunlight as they prepare for redolent summer heat.

We have lost this day an opportunity to perform
our poems in person.

Through atmospheric cloud and mist,
I seek the moon as evening rises.

From the Confines of a Work Table

Their sentences lengthen
in the realm of forgotten

imprisoned words
and random thoughts

once precious
now merely juvenile.

What's to become of them
in their faded beauty,

in their discarded state
as chaff

but to grind them
to a fine powder,

dissolve each line
into a cook's hash,

their bulk to enhance
the subtle spice

of other words
and release them all

into a palatable
taste-tested feast.

Old School Library

In the room
without a clock,
walnut shelves line

each paneled wall
floor to ceiling,
around and inside

cushioned window seats
dressed in natural light.
Rolling ladders give

access to each book,
their spines colorful
as grocery displays

of packaged foods
and new produce,
some more palatable

than others,
full of prophesy,
history and fantasy.

Philosophical thoughts
click, grind, bang
against silence

like revelers
who celebrate
the end of dull

days, and time
just another concept,
not a constraint.

Divorce

Staple by staple, she forces each one out
with a chisel, blade dull and worn,

to separate the frame from its canvas
and though the wood splinters a bit,

it holds firm its centuries-old form.
The material frays at attachment points.

Once a pure surface in white gesso,
the new marriage of shapes and colors

develops too many fault lines
and no longer holds upright its image

of a bent tree's thick base strong enough
to grow toward the sun's illumination.

Untethered she rolls up the painting,
stores it in some non-weather-proof unit

allows it to fade and crack further
and like her other failures,

time completes the dissolution
along with any memory of it.

Waiting

Today's task is to sort debris,
remove canvas beneath wire coils
snug as serpents hibernating
during an extended winter.

From a pile of feathers, I imagine
hair ornaments for women intrepid
as the smokey blue jays
from which they fell.

And maybe the crows silky black
might form a cape, shoulder to heel
with red macaw plumage on its collar.

It would be easier
to paint these images
than weave them by hand.

They wait for what I thought to be
a couple of weeks, become a month,
then two, three and now, no clear reprieve.

The fear of permanent confinement
haunts me at night. A coastal fog
dims the light I want to rise each morning,

clouds the promise of a fresh day, sameness
filtered to drab. The dropped corners
of my mouth hide behind colorful masks

as if the patterns represent hope,
and my organized workspace contains
items necessary for a someday open future.

The Process

The trash bag grows heavy
as it bulges with discarded slides,
those pieces of celluloid
in plastic frames, or cardboard,
which is the better choice
upon which to write
artist-title-medium-size,
since labels peel, jam the projector,
another item we no longer need
with computer technology,
its ephemeral storage of images.

The discards click
an old newsreel
of my past artworks.
Memory rolls out
how strong my fingers were,
my hands thick, muscular
from the energy
I worked into clay
or onto canvas,

and the many photographers
I hired, each with a particular style.
One serious about his work,
another with a roguish smile,
preferred payment in artwork.
But one especially dear,
the mother of nine children.
I marveled how she maneuvered
her camera bags, lights,
umbrellas and stands upstairs
to my studio, photographed work
with such attentive care.
She already understood
our creations were to be savored,
documented, and with grace,
allowed to leave.

II

Planting Mint and Roses

Katherine

Your face brightens with a smile when we enter your room
        and tears well up, flow slowly
                from the corners of your eyes.

For the moment, I think you may be happy
        to see me, not just your sons
                but you can barely speak
                        for all the congestion in your chest

until you notice your name penned on the wall chart,
        repeating it again and again,
                the repetition says everything
                you cannot.

We three sit with you for a long hour
        talking about our children
                and the political events of the day.
                        You try to follow, even participate

but fade into your own thoughts from time to time
        with an unwrinkled brow
                and the smooth face of one
                        who floats in peaceful slumber.

Your white hair, auburn in your fiery years,
        then a superior blonde
                when I married your son,
                        now purified with age and dementia,

curls along your cheek, its silk a kiss
        while the late afternoon sun graces your forehead,
                shines in your eyes,
                      and you bask in its warm light.

Four O'clock Somewhere

The lonely hours begin to set long before the sun
          when I have nowhere to meet friends in person.

This is the time my mother once spoke of sadness,
          the day almost done, too early for supper.

She would sit on the porch steps, eyes into the sun
          as if she expected it to not abandon her yet again

to an unrequited love she could not name, but if asked,
          she would begin a litany.

In what has become known as the time of covid-19,
          I search the television channels for news,

salve myself with a glass of wine and pretend
          I have company.

Were she alive today, I would gather her in my arms
          like a bouquet of fragrant lilies and roses.

We would share our stories
          and she would understand.

The Immigrant's Daughter

She cried when you were born,
not because you were a girl,
though that was a disappointment,

but with relief and joy in language
strange to the hospital staff.
Your mother had no teeth,

vestige from a childhood of war
and a dentist whose disdain
outweighed his clinical judgment:

he had pulled them all.
Thus, her dentures slipped out
during the turmoil of labor.

She wailed and tried to run
until a blitz of belladonna
made her docile for the duration.

When nurses washed your body,
taut from its confinement,
your skin broke into a rash

like a sprouted potato
crowned in lush dark hair.
At home, your tiny cries attracted

the widow across the street
who offered to babysit
since she needed money

and cared for other children.
She was Lakota-Sioux-Pawnee,
dressed in freckles, red hair

and Navaho turquoise, gifts
from her German-born father;
it was she who taught you to speak.

Matins

in morning moonlight
cool air on our faces

the hint of sunrise
through tinted clouds

we two walk east
in step
mother with daughter

our capable hands
move with purpose

when we plant roses
and water mint

Prelude

I know one day
you will go away,
      but I hold you this moment.
      You are water.
            I drink quickly.

It says somewhere
in contemporary scripture
      I must help you buy
      clothes to pack,
            provide the suitcase.

I must purchase
your travel,
      pay your tuition,
      guide your departure
            as I guided your first steps.

Your eagerness, fear and trust,
encircle you now as then.
      For this, too,
      I proffer myself
            unquenched.

Persephone's Testament

I carry armloads of wild lilies
and lupine
        to market,

my mother already there
with her bundles
        of wheat.

As I approach the merchant's stall
a man emerges
        from the shadows,

his long dark curls and luminous eyes
mesmerize me.
        He offers a pomegranate
                plump, luscious.

I taste the seeds, their juice sweet
as it runs down
        past my chin.

His whispers become kisses
on my ear, my throat
        between my breasts

to the red pool
gathered at my navel
        and beyond.

I open myself to him
and when he enters me
        I know I will be queen.

Afterward

this house
so empty

the walls echo
silence

without
        your wit
        your laughter

        the light
        through your curls

                an amber lace
                in ebony hair

morning sun
merciless

in your absence
makes the air

heavy
with what is

The Immigrant Mother

Her wild hair catches the sun
as she gathers bunches of mint,
leaves the garden hose

to continue a trickle of water
most living things require
in the desert heat.

She washes her harvest,
lays the cuttings on cotton sheets
as infants down to nap.

It takes a few days in dry air
for leaves to become flakes
she crumbles into jars

that will last for decades,
gifts to her children
as photographs of times past

though they may not appreciate it now,
like that daughter who rarely visits.
What does this child know of loneliness?

She had a babysitter as an infant
and later, the privilege of going to school.
Even if she came home to an empty house,

made her own dinner; she had food and
clothes her mother worked to provide.
Though the girl had to ride a city bus,

her instructions were to sit next to the driver.
Her mother warned about lascivious men
in the context of her father's affairs,

a subject she tried to impart once
to her daughter's daughter,
but was interrupted by the distrust

she reaped from her previous lectures
no dried mint would assuage,
its bitterness persistent.

Portraiture

It captured a rare moment,
one in which she smiled,
  this photograph of her as a warm,
  receptive mother from 1950's television.

I treasured this gentle image,
meticulously copied it,
  transferred my drawing
  onto wood blocks to carve

but as I began, the delicate lines
of her face became deeper,
  lips pursed, eyes opened too wide,
  and the initial prints harsh

as contemporary portraits of a fierce woman,
a concept she held of herself and her *lady friends*
  adorned in fancy clothes,
  their weight in jewelry,

permed and colored hair,
lips slathered in bright lipsticks
  at lunches, with coffee, pastries,
  full of laughter and judgments.

With oil pastels, I made the images rich
in textured color and proudly pinned up five
  on the wall in preparation for her visit
  to my house and studio.

She carefully inspected each room.
You have no pictures of me.
  I am your mother.
  You should have one.

After she left, I collected the prints into a folder
with layers of tissue in between,
> placed them in my file drawer
> for unsold work.

Bittersweet Chocolate

Sweet but not sweet enough,
those memories of mother,
compared to the dove
who warms her nest

and never moves until
she must find food
for her hatchlings
in the kind of devotion

she talked about but sat
deep in her imagination.

Today is the anniversary
of my mother's death,
her physical one
and though her memory

never leaves me,
conscious or unconscious,
I harbor her lessons
from the voyage here

through threatening storms
and endless horizons
of tumulous waves.
Her fiancé abandoned,

she arrived in bracelets
and red lipstick,
her suitcase packed
with empty dresses.

March Winds

When she mispronounces
a word or misspeaks a phrase,
      she laughs with her children
      to hide frustration at her tongue
            awkward in new sounds
            from her adopted language.

Once she reaches her humor's limit,
her standard lecture begins,
      how she speaks and reads
      and writes two languages,
            studies each in evening classes
            while they only manage one.

When they roll eyes and smirk,
her retorts come at them interspersed
      with insults and swear words,
      a mother crow who caws
            at her offspring
            surrounded by broken shells,

the old culture stillborn
when her children fly
      on the currents of now
      untethered to traditions
            she accommodates
            but also flees.

A Wedding Portrait

Delicate white flowers lace the edges of her veil as it flows
along her dress, folds upon itself at her feet,

next to my father who stands in a dark grey suit,
his hands already large from labor,

their faces young and full but serious.
Few people smiled in the days of the Great Depression.

Were they in love, happy that day, these two people
recently introduced and encouraged to marry?

They survived starvation and orphanhood in the First World War,
crossed an ocean, navigated a new language

with an alphabet moving in a different direction, no hint
of future hunger, the death of their first-born son.

By the time I came into their lives, their faces were thin,
weathered by the desert sun, eyes and bodies weary

from tending customers in their grocery, laughter dormant
until they retired and became family elders.

How could they have known, any more than my husband and I,
what decades bring? Did they have the same moment of panic I had

as I began to walk down the aisle, and was there someone
like my father who, with firm hand, said, *let's go, it will be fine*?

Ordinary Dad

He may not ponder his insistence on whole wheat bread
as opposed to cinnamon toast at breakfast

nor the laundry that never seems done while he wears
dribbled egg yolk on his shirt.

He pays last month's electric bill on the computer
with the lights turned on,

parses each child's screen time until
they watch basketball games together.

When the temperature reaches ninety degrees,
he leaves the air conditioner on,

takes his son and daughter
for chocolate ice cream and strawberry popsicles.

They may not remember the everyday cereals
any more than a house remembers

its bricks and boards after the drywall goes up
but as a builder, he knows the placement

of each nail and slab of mortar
when the owners need an appraisal.

The Passing

The boys buried their dog
beneath a juvenile pine,

made a mosaic plaque
to mark his grave.

After bedtime rituals
of brushed teeth and a storybook

with lights out and door closed,
the younger one cried with abandon,

while the older one became quiet,
gave one-word answers,

continued to read his book,
feelings as vibrant

as a painter's palette
momentarily secured

with the watercolors
in his desk drawer.

Inland Cruise

Laughter and lies
at the dinner table,

jovial face of a man
with an oncology

appointment who
celebrates his birthday

three weeks early
among new best friends,

an ocean of wine,
jibes and jokes,

and his wife gracious
in her frozen smile.

A man

stands at age twenty-three
exposed to sun, rain, neglect
in a grove of lemon trees
behind rows of Camellias
where flocks of birds
spend their winter

"Mama, don't leave me here"

"I cannot care for you, son
I am too fragile

Your sister will feed you
and later, she will cry
over your grave

She carries a mother's heart"

I search stone markers
for names of ancestors
the recent ones I did not meet

the one who dies too soon
the one in the photograph
who holds me at age three
in his muscular arms
his handsome face and smile
say he knows love

but I have no memory of him

"Cousins find you in the yard
unconscious and think
perhaps you are drunk

Later they discover
a blood vessel ruptured
in your brain"

"Your sister spoons life and memory
into your mouth
until you can no longer
bear either"

During the lemon harvest
when Camellias bloom their finest
among abundant birdsong
he would have turned twenty-nine

Swimmer

Blustery waters dissolve the line
        between clouds and sea.

Thunderstorms care nothing
        for him, or anyone.

Their rains sustain
        only this ocean.

No longer content
        in his seasoned solitude,

he paces the coast.
        Wet sand sinks

beneath his footsteps,
        coats his skin

while he calculates his journey,
        fills his lungs with air

and begins the arduous swim,
        though he cannot be certain

where he will land
        or whether he will.

Reunion

Changes rolled in
on a tumbleweed's path

until they gathered against the fence
around his childhood home,

one metal building behind it
crowded by another structure,

no room left for the apricot trees
nor the trellis of grapevines

that provided summer shade.
He thought he lost himself

not just his youth
when he grew old enough

to leave that house
now with bars on its windows

against gangs of roving crimes,
his grief shared by neighbors

who also moved to other places
and where he, too, learned

to savor photographs as artifacts
in a personal museum.

Mirror, Mirror

He claims to be weary.

His persona cracks brittle
as dried mud.

Why not revel in a face
of soft worn leather?

But who would notice?

Settled-in age
makes him invisible

in dust transparent
as parchment

or goatskin on a drum
with brown rivulets

or the skin covering
red blue travel routes

on his worn and varicose legs.

Dandelion

His headwaters
nourish this weed
with yellow flowers
children gather
into bouquets.
It hibernates
in snow,
anticipates rain
to flourish again
from ancestor roots
in deep earth
diligent
resilient
persistent
spreads leaves
of jagged petals
into luxurious verdance,
sometimes for salads
and wine.
Cactus strong
in dry heat,
its puff white seeds
flow on mere wind,
sprinkle the ground
to renew
lush blooms
the way guilts
strengthen
on the slightest
of his failures
to meet his mother's
continuous requests
for his presence
and praise
but primitively
for the power

to manage
his future work,
his wife and progeny.

Apologia

You sing
a young tenor's aria

in a series of playful chords,
a canary in want of company.

Too soon it gives way
to a blue jay's strident squawk.

You refuse to accommodate
anyone upon approach,

as if you are majesty
required to protect your domain.

On the bridge between
morning and night

we share our bewilderment
until lightning arcs

from the depth of your eyes.
Your storm returns and thunder reigns.

You were once a little bird
waiting for its mother's worms,

the mother who always came to you,
who, then one day, didn't.

Runaways

They run in the dark
middle of their road

edged in sweet
berry brambles.

They devour the fruit
by handfuls.

It stains mouths
blue-black,

thorns scratch
palms, fingers,

ankles crisscross red.
Eager for warmth

they find an empty
tent, by moonlight,

beneath the overpass
enter, zip it closed

unaware
the resident spider

may be poisonous,
their only concern

its intricate weavings
cover them.

Migration

He became tiresome, this companion
   who lost his charm by nesting too long

like the persistent odor of cod cooked
   in a fisherman's cabin,

or camembert crusted on the cheese board
   after last night's party

along with beer gone flat.

She wanted to sleep past noon, awake slowly
   into a clean place, windows opened

by a housekeeper who tossed out the spoils
   and washed all her dishes.

She pulled up the blinds, gathered his clothes,
   set them on the curb.

With no hangover, she searched her contacts
   for options.

Unsheltered Within

When you toss your jacket
on the sofa where I usually
rest to watch television,

the line between love
and ownership
wavers.

I fill your cookie jar daily.
You tend the roses,
my vase abundant in fragrance.

All with provisions:
thorns must be snipped
before you enter the house

where my oven temperature
remains moderately set
to a careful timer.

We sustain each other
in sweetness and flowers,
certain only of this day,

and leave the sprinklers on,
nurture our grassy yard
from encroaching sands.

For there is no water
in a virtual oasis.
Only mirage.

How else are we to manage
this desert without the verdance
of children and friends?

A question,
one of many here,
with no foreseeable answer.

Succession

In the days after the funeral
        and a montage
        of captured moments,
                smiles and perfect poses,
                        old memories linger.

Clouds come and go like phases of grief,
        some benign,
        others moisture-laden
                and dark with a sense
                        of the ominous.

My sister and I must find a new arrangement.
                We are now matriarchs who sound the depths
                for how to live this next phase
                        as if truths reside in a turquoise pool
                                where water reflects the sky.

Stillness becomes an art we must create
                in spite of our need for physical presence,
                tuned to the slow beats of a heart
                        and the breath in, then out,
                        while the mind rests

on a single item, perhaps a rose,
        its modulate colors deepen
        from stem to petal edge,
                thorns a lighter hue
                        to catch our attention,

warn us of their potential pain.
        We may admire but not touch,
        for this is a process,
                its acceptance
                      determined by will.

Poolside

The boy trains for his future swim meet with other
aquatic bodies agile as dolphins.

The familiar scent of pool water, slaps of feet
on wet cement, fill the air.

Something I should remember from long times past
begins to surface.

Where I am now seems like a movie
I watch for the first time

in which I must assess the characters,
pay no attention to my sepia mood.

I don't know how to do this any better
with evening sunburst in my eyes

after my clouds empty themselves for this hour
while I wait to bring him home.

Redress

no matter the meaning
        her words come
        rapid as gun fire

while she wears her woes
        snug to her bosom
        in an expensive tee shirt

scooped low enough
        for the pierced heart
        on her tanned breast

to reveal cracks
        wide as the ones
        in old sidewalks

through which weeds grow
        their roots ju-jitsu
        for dominance

neither tools nor fingers can release
        only poison that dissolves
        with each season

according to the gardener who says
        they must be destroyed
        as enemies in a war

but even the vanquished
        lie in wait
        for opportunity

and they grow back
        deep as shame
        inflicted by classmates

or a mom or dad
     no therapist can remove
     only teach her to step over

III

Eye of A Wanderer

Specter

The sky burns orange
in a seared memory,

the vision once real
appears against

a cloudless
May morning

in anticipation
of few rains.

All winter I hunger
for these Sierras

with their vistas
of thick pines

and granite peaks,
trees fragrant

as snow
succumbs to sun,

and winds that
brush pine needles

into hymns,
a treasure

an errant spark
of lightning

can consume
into choking ash.

Summer Redux

The horror ignites
with a tiny crackle,
transforms itself
into a wild creature
that races across ground,
expands wider and higher
until it engulfs
the entire scene.

The fire generates
its own wind,
loud as a train roaring
through tunnels,
whips up, then down
into an unholy swirl,
consumes everything,
so intense,
sky bends light.

All kneel, curl,
disappear into ash,
bitter evidence
of this cruel act.

Mountain Morning

Startled awake by vivid dreams,
the kind that plagues me at high altitude:

all I hold precious dissolves into air.
My dog greets me with a thump of tail,

his eyes barely open after I cup his head
and rub his flanks. He follows me

to my favorite chair, lies down beside it,
lifts his head and rests it on his paws,

watches me watch sky turn from grey
to orange as light crests the peaks,

 turn again from yellow to cream.
Hints of clear sky streak pale

through stayed clouds
transparent as layers of thin ice.

Pine branches glow green to gold,
their needles and cones shimmer

while fragrant drops of moisture
slowly evaporate in simple quiet.

We can hike trails to celebrate
no fires today, not yet.

Boy in A Pine Forest

He climbs up the rocks
and proclaims his expertise

on top a boulder three times
higher than himself

jumps down and kicks
pine cones onto the trail

practices his balance skills
on each fallen log

scampers off-trail to explore
with no regard for deer or bear

nor the fragrance from lodgepoles and firs
the warm sun bestows on us

waters a tree like the mountain man
he determines to be

catches us at the bridge
to watch a tumultuous flow

into Twin Lakes and share
our thrill of high vistas

as wafts of campfire breakfasts
compete with his dream

of flight down the waterfall
with the glide of a raptor.

A Storm in August

Across the sky sidewinder streaks
        glow as if infused
                with radioactive dye.

Vibrating veins feed capillaries
        white serum electricity,
                spurs erratic attacks into earth,

which responds the way
        coiled rattlesnakes leap to inject
                a deadly venom into intruders.

Whole regions light up
        in multiple strikes splayed to form
                an arterial map of quick-flash pathways.

Thunder arrives
        in a clap and roll sequence
                behind tumbles of gravid clouds.

The rare torrent
        might settle summer's dust,
                cause reptiles to hide.

But lightning resumes its frenzy,
        heat dissipates the moisture
                before it reaches ground.

Late Summer Blues

Daylight comes early before
I am ready to face another day

of grass golden
in summer sunrise,

the color of wheat
and plants burnt rust,

then dusty pale
in endless afternoon.

Sparrows and blue jays
seem content

to feast
on buried worms

abundant in spite of heat,
but hide among tree leaves

until the sun angles
toward horizon.

I am impatient for rain
whether as drizzle

or in torrents
matters not,

only that the earth
becomes verdant again.

Miner's Cabin

It nestles
       in filigreed shade
       bravely rooted

among ancient pines
       first annoyed
       at the disruption

from this intruder
       into their tranquil side
       of a mountain indifferent

to whether such a homestead,
       with its corrugated roof
       and stone fireplace,

withstands snow,
       ice too cold to melt
       or summer fires,

rain and earthquake,
       built of cedar
       in the newborn color

of reddish brown,
       now a seasoned silver,
       chameleon against the bark

of trees whose branches
       spread themselves
       to shelter it

as a secret solace
       to the percipient eye
       of a wanderer.

September Afternoon

Crisp autumn light drapes
      the Buddha's shoulders

as if it is still summer
      and heat radiates an aura

the colors of sun,
      pale yellow gold,

on verdant bamboo leaves
      warm, moist,

their fragrance
      one can almost taste.

Light wind creates shadows
      across amber tiles

molded in perfect squares,
      contrast his round body,

its bronze form rigidly cast
      somewhere in Japan,

a foundry
      for tourist export

to encourage a firm
      stillness of mind

for those who listen
      to silence.

September Lament

The day's heat lingers after the sun sets into orange clouds.
      It is late September, mornings still hot,

the pond ripe with algae. Even as summer delays its departure,
      geese gather in time for the thrust south,

They cluster on abundant grass, feast on resident insects
      to fortify themselves,

a port to collect their group before the alphas honk
      instruction to five or sometimes nine members.

Each distinctive call continues through arrowed flights
      as if to cheer the way home.

Mementos left along walkways wait for next seasons rains,
      no owners to clean them up.

I am eager for autumn, sun angled toward brilliance,
      cool air in the afternoon.

Eager, too, for snow on spruce, clear night skies,
      holy communion with the north star.

Lundy Canyon on My Cousin's Birthday

October slips in quietly
    first one leaf, then two or three
        their yellow comradery spreads
        into golden quivers soft
           amid pine needles hush

a performance interrupted
    by too many photographers
        who crowd narrow roads
        hope to capture the sun's dance
           on shimmering leaves

in the one photo among thousands taken
    which brings fame
        and another paid assignment
        about these aspens' age
           their family of roots

nearly ancient as the mountain river
    along which they thrive
        in colors like the burst of flame
        when fire ignites

We once hiked the strenuous trails
    at the top of this canyon,
        celebrated our young bodies
        autumnal years far from mind

Now we shiver in the cool wind
    warm ourselves in sunlight
        when it calms
        as if the weather
           can't decide which to be

But we know
    it will succumb yet again
        to the mountains' call for change

the promised rain soon
      followed by whispered flurries
      of dry Sierra snow

North Light

Clouds hover
over miles of Mojave Desert
      with intermittent downpours,
      their silver-white dances
      glide over lakes,
            hide distant mountains
            then reshape their images
            in turbulent wind.

We follow an old road
and an ancient trail
      as we climb
      into a pine forest,
      upper branches
            in constant mist
            more pale teal
            than green,

to our mountain lodge,
where its fireplace crackles,
      its tall windows
      open vistas
      of fir trees among
            feather-leaf cedars
            and glimpses
            of an evening sun.

Refuge at Mono Lake

Gulls glide in fine feathers
        sleek against their white bodies.

They skim waves for enough food
        to cast themselves on high currents,

breach mountains, search for their inland
        sea ripe with brine shrimp

and old nests tucked in tufa crevices,
        stark and porous,

safe from fox or coyote,
        monitored by great horned owls.

The Sonora

Snow lights crevices in a saguaro forest;
    arms reach through cold,
        wait for sunrise to crest the hill.

    It mounds against the cholla
        across already-white plains
        and long indentations of rock mesas,
            striations coated for a few hours
            until the sun's zenith, when every cactus
    absorbs the moisture into itself.

Still, variations of pale remain, compliments
    of ultra-violet rays that bleach color
    from all they see. Primordial salts gather
        in ancient puddles and dried creek beds
        where the earth curls slices of ash colored mud
    and rain so rare it measures a mere few inches.

Fires will not burn this terrain,
    but the desert sustains no angel.
        It tests the most holy;
            stones resemble bread
            and light masquerades as water.

The courageous, or sometimes, the mystical,
    wander this ground to commune
        with its eternal warmth,
    to decipher runes carved
        by those who walked here
        before their bones scattered,
            and through which cacti grow.

Wild Horse

Bone white ribs,
a hint of brown fur
rest tattered at the site

of half-eaten, half-rotten innards,
face intact, one eye gone,
the other, black glass,

stench like processed jerky
in a makeshift kiln
fired by the Mojave sun.

In this ravine,
coffin-recesses welcome
any animal whose slipped hoof

breaks a femur
and soft sand draws
its body down,

its plight a footnote
in ancestral history:
a lone Equus

searches for water
but fooled by a hillside
weak from flash floods

struggles to climb out,
finds its final destiny
a scavenger's cornucopia.

Olive Branch

A dove flies into
my studio window,
with tail and wings
fanned in flight,
sunlight on the tips
of its feathers
in a symphony
of whites, soft grays
and memories
of its singular melody.

When doves coo
in the morning,
I become a child
awakening to avian sounds
as they warm themselves
over telephone lines
against a brilliant sky,
musicians and
easy targets.

In the garage,
my mother's back to me,
her pale green dress
tied with a gingham apron,
she labors removing feathers
from my brother's cache.
I ask why

he killed the doves.
She complains
of so much effort
for barely a morsel,
terminates his escapades
after a wayward bone
pierces her hand.
To my young mind,

these are Noah's doves,
one, a divine messenger
to the weary ark of pairs.

Eugenics

Mechanized arms seize each tree,
rip its roots from the earth
and toss it into heaps slated for mulch.
       Bees swarm
       around wilted flowers
       and oranges left to rot.

Birds' lungs burn from an argument
between the tractor's wheels
and ochre dirt,
       unable to swallow
       what they glean
       in the midst of invasion.

When dust clears,
they rant at the driver
who walks beside his labors,
       head held high
       as if to taunt
       the residents he displaces.

I once observed crows
chase a Redtail hawk
into another murder,
       a scene repeating itself
       from one cluster to another
       until the predator relents.

This driver shelters in his vehicle,
reviews his plan for a vineyard
covered in bird-resistant nets,
       water rights reclaimed,
       his quest for profit
       secure.

Pas de Deux

A pair of willows
sentinel the bridge across

a seasonal stream
lined with mossy grey stones.

In late winter they present
a nude symmetry

of exposed branches
with tips of green promise.

Some limbs bow graciously,
others sway upward

and when the leaves return,
these stems flutter

skirts of fine tulle between
substance and filtered light.

The trees become a lattice
 of two resilient individuals,

through the choreography
of storms and drought,

their roots a web
of inseparable threads.

Yet, a premonition hovers
with one tree's brittle boughs,

unleafed and pale as it awaits
pruning shears, then curatives,

stark against its lush spring costume,
a dance elder couples know well.

The Coffee Table

The feast begins with coffee
and a few flakes from raisin toast,
a dawn of caffeine and sugar
to light the day.
Later come tasty remnants
of popcorn, hot cocoa,
sticky juices and tiny morsels
of secreted chocolate,

all to be graciously wiped away
by that diligent sweeper—
the dog's pernicious tongue,
though it can barely reach
the current accumulation
of cookie crumbs in each corner
where the glass surface
sits in wood.

Some hidden drops of ice cream
and various debris
decorate the area rug beneath,
too fancy for a play room
but no one minds,
any child is welcome
with a smidgen of imagination
and his canine partner

to the table piled high
with Lego space stations
and elaborate ships
flown by fantastic creatures
through galaxies
beyond our own
in search of adventures
where good always prevails.

Early morning

thoughts run amok
like children at recess
I curl into my pillow
not ready to face dawn
seductive bed
cradles me
warm
soft
molded to my body
as a tender lover
post orgasmic

But coffee promises
an aromatic burst
of energy
focus

Newspaper waits at the end
of a long driveway
wet
from unauthorized sprinklers
and news of killings
in bold print
singular
and mass
make me yearn
for the few
moments
ago

Beneath Monet's Garden

Who thinks of lily roots
except racoons
hungry for fish hidden
in these underwater webs,
mere obstructions
easily whisked away
by dexterous paws?

Not the blue heron
whose sharp eyes
monitor higher
than drones,
its advantage
speed and razer beak
should a fish weave
upward to feast
on mosquitos
and thirsty flies.

Beneath green pads
tadpoles incubate
on food attached
to rhizome strands
along the pond's
muddy bottom,
its surface replete
with luscious blooms,
distractions from
lethal competition
in this apparent,
tranquil scene.

Acoustical Polyphony in Election Season

In high grass, rattlesnakes
      warn against intruders,
            their tails in rapid syncopation.

Ranchers need live horses and goats,
      not discarded-metal-and-old-board pretenders,
            popular among wanna-be country folk,

but those made of fur and flesh with hooves,
      muscular snouts in front of flat-edged teeth,
            precision designed, superior
                  to any automated mower.

Goats plea for attention between
      nibbles of grass and weeds in a corral
            where the mare waits for grain, kicks
                  her heels, races to nicker her demands,

when the sheep dog barks orders at her.
      Chickens cluck their way
            into an orchard for dropped fruit breakfasts
                after donating eggs to the food supply.

Quail and pheasant coveys chatter
      beneath blackberry brambles
            along a summer stream to feast
                in a preserve of wild plants and insects.

Geese celebrate in raucous clusters
      around a pond until uncollared dogs
            chase them though they leave
                smelly deposits before flight.

From the house once a barn
      local residents watch at midnight
            for a mountain lion seen
                on hidden cameras in thick brush,

but only coyote and racoon appear
  agile, clever and hungry enough
    to thwart efforts against them.

Wood and iron fences articulate properties
  where prey hide in chicken coops
    or enclosed gardens once darkness settles.

For a few night hours, quiet reigns, moments count
  until a singular rooster crows at daybreak,
    winner claims all.

Catfish

A current news feed
flashes on his phone,

eyebrows raise then curl
with talk of scandal

against his favorite congressman
with which our friend disagrees.

Conversations bubble
into argument until

a waiter serves our dinner,
the day's catch.

Catfish loom large on our plates,
heads curved toward us,

tails hang over the edge
in fragrant ginger sauce,

silver skin glistens crisp
over tender flesh

tucked between flexible bones.
We want to know

what nourishes it.
Pheasants eat bugs and worms.

Mushrooms grow in horse dung
and this fish, a bottom-feeder

on what settles in dark riverbeds,
restaurants prefer it farm-raised

where food, unlike his politics,
generates a palatable flavor.

Assaulted Wound

Prometheus, the creator of mankind...gave (them) fire...
The Greek Myths by Robert Graves

Prometheus, the gods are angry, vengeful, but you know that.
        Only now we, too, suffer their punishments.

Zeus throws down magnificent lightning, though more
        than our earth can handle.

Tree after tree ignites until forests, already weakened
        by beetle appetites, crisp and turn black.

Poseidon drowns our shores with endless storms, hurricanes,
        cyclones, each one devastating as he forces sea water

inland, its salt dissolves soil nutrients, new foliage will not grow.
        Houses collapse, sodden wood disintegrates.

Demeter withholds her fecund fields, allows Helios
        to dry golden grass into tinder, her rage worse

than when Hades stole her daughter. Zeus brokered a deal
        for Persephone's return of half a year,

but no Olympian solution appears regardless of our supplications.
        Perhaps, dear savior, you suffer more to see us,

the ones for whom you sacrificed your freedom, squander your gift,
        mine the earth, poison waters, darken the air.

Perhaps you see we mortals are infatuated with our ingenuity,
        and in your image, remain dumb to its consequences.

A Week Before the Election

Autumn, cool almost cold, but no rain, out of season
as it is everywhere.

Winds rage, our nation rages. Even the virus rages.
In the west, we pray that no more fires ravage our forests.

Everywhere else, we pray no fires enflame our streets.
But we all know ignition is already in process.

First a lie, then more, then an entire sky full
of embers fall to earth, scatter flames

worse than lightning, which only strikes one place.
Sparks carry all through cities, over open fields

into each person's thoughts, including children,
who see the source, wonder at the cause.

We pray for rain to quell winter ash before it spreads
across the continent into our lungs

and frozen particles make us too ill to stand up
and sweep it out of our homes.

In the Eye of the Storm

Votes are still being counted forty-eight hours
after the designated day for elections to end.

A hurricane out at sea threatens landfall in its previous
port, but turns toward another further west,

the place ancient cultures claim as the direction of death,
perhaps because that is where they see the sun rest

or disappear, and it requires rituals to assuage the storm,
according to the sophistication of their storytellers.

Surely, they know it rises again come morning, earth
and sky fresh with new light, dew and replenishing mist,

all that we hope benevolent gods will bestow upon us
when we mark our ballots for the future of our dreams,

protection from floods and rains of unwanted politics.
Anticipation with simultaneous fear and hope,

requires we, too, be calm in the face of it.

Geese again

surround the pond, out of season, as is the sun.
Mid-December feels like early fall.

Did they return or never leave, merely rest at the local
sanctuary, along with egrets and Sandhill cranes

who normally winter there? The cold remains elusive,
an unkept promise. Insects and worms thrive.

The birds sit quietly along the shore, nestled among reeds,
burnt ocher from winter heat,

no longer in exuberant gaggles feasting
to fatten themselves for long migrations south.

So much seems out of place that I wonder if there will be
spring spiders in January and summer ants in February.

My concern seeps like fouled water into stream beds
that feed this small lake. I cannot know what they feel,

but they seem content in their opportunity to wait
until they figure out how to live with these changes.

Meanwhile, Mallards paddle nearby, gather
to pair and nest.

Acknowledgements

I would like to thank the editors of the following literary journals where these poems first appeared, sometimes in earlier versions.

Becomings Collective: "The Artists Circle"
                          "The Process"
Door Is A Jar: "Old School Library"
Ginosko Literary Journal: "A Storm in August"
                          "Heritage"
                          "Mountain Morning"
                          "Summer Redux"
Gold Country Writers Chapbook: "Olive Branch"
Inlandia: A Literary Journal: "Bittersweet Chocolate"
                          "Redress"

Literary Alchemy Press,
The Poetry and Fiction Zine: "Reservoir"
Muddy River Poetry Review: "Wild Horse"
Plainsongs: "The Coffee Table"
Poetry Quarterly: "Katherine"
San Pedro River Review: "The Sonora"
                          "Miner's Cabin"

Southwestern American
Literature: "The Immigrant Mother"
                          "The Immigrant's Daughter"
Spectrum: "Persephone's Testament"
                          "In Rilke's Shadow"

I am deeply grateful to the Ravens Poetry Workshop, the many poets, friends and family for their inspiration, encouragement and critical evaluation.

Georgette Unis is the author of *Tremors*, a chapbook of poems published by Finishing Line Press in 2018. Several literary journals have published her poetry such as *Naugatuck River Review, San Pedro River Review, Southwestern American Literature* and *Ginosko Literary Review.*

In addition to her work as a poet, she has an MFA in mixed media painting and has exhibited her artwork in many solo and group exhibitions, where some galleries have presented broadsides of her poems.

Though born and raised in Arizona, she fell in love with the Sierras in California where she has lived most of her life. The mountains, forests and deserts leading to them, set the stage for the complex relationships between people that inspire both her literary and visual work.

She maintains her home and studio in the Sierra foothills of northern California where she lives with her husband of fifty years.